AFRICAN WRITERS SERIES
Founding editor • Chinua Achebe

Igbo Traditional Verse

compiled and translated by

ROMANUS EGUDU
and
DONATUS NWOGA

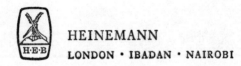

HEINEMANN
LONDON · IBADAN · NAIROBI

Heinemann Educational Books Ltd
48 Charles Street London WIX 8AH
P.M.B. 5205 Ibadan. P.O. BOX 45314 Nairobi
EDINBURGH MELBOURNE TORONTO
NEW DELHI AUCKLAND HONG KONG
SINGAPORE KUALA LUMPUR

ISBN 0 435 90129 X
© in translations, selection and introduction
Romanus N. Egudu and Donatus I. Nwoga 1971
and 1973

First published under the title *Poetic Heritage* by
Nwankwo-Ifejika & Co., Enugu, Nigeria, 1971
First published in African Writers Series 1973

The Nigerian edition has been accepted in the Nigerian
Translations Series of the United Nations Educational,
Scientific and Cultural Organisation (UNESCO)

Printed in England by Cox & Wyman Ltd,
London, Reading and Fakenham

CONTENTS

PREFACE   Igbo vernacular poetry in both its traditional and current forms has never had the publicity or exposition it merits by its intrinsic nature as poetry of high quality and as an expression of a people's history, their varied beliefs and their states of mind and emotion. This anthology is a first attempt to fill this regrettable gap.

The poems collected here come from a variety of locations ranging from Udi in Northern Igboland to the Owerri and Ngwa areas in the South. They cover recitations, songs from women's and men's groups and dances. They deal with philosophical and sometimes mystic reflections on life and nature, penetrating comments on social and political events, and praise and criticism of society and persons. The moods range from the serious to the light-hearted.

This book will be found invaluable by general readers but more specifically by scholars, teachers, and students of African literature.

It might be questioned by what criteria we include
contemporary verse on life and persons which obviously
has been composed in the last few years within the
'traditional', since 'traditional' is normally understood
to mean the product of a forgotten past, handed down
from generations immemorial. We do this because our
concept of 'traditional' has as its antithesis 'modern'
and both are separated in the African context not so
much by time as by mentality and mode. The mode
that distinguishes the modern from the traditional in
this context is whether the verse belongs to the written
tradition or to the oral tradition. The verses in this
collection belong to the oral tradition of the Igbo.

They were composed according to the social (cul-
tural or ceremonial) needs of the communities, from
literary material and according to the traditional form
deriving from and indigenous to the communities.
They have not been influenced in any vital sense by
literary forms and techniques which have been intro-
duced through formal education. The forms of com-
position are still traditional whether they come from the
areas of ritual and ceremony and have been handed in
exact formulations down the generations or are new
compositions belonging to transitory dance forms and
commenting on the most contemporary social issue.
In another context somebody has defined traditional in
the African situation as 'denoting the fantastic pattern
of institutions deriving from the pre-colonial period
and still remarkably persistent'. (P. C. Lloyd, *Africa in
Social Change*, Penguin, 1969, pp. 12-13.)

There are 'modern' Igbo verses composed by
educated individuals in the privacy of their study for
use by church choirs or for publication. These have
not been included in this collection.

(a) *The Oral Presentation*

It has already been indicated that the verses published here were collected from the oral rather than the written tradition. It is important to recognize the nature of the influence which this has on the appreciation of the words in the text. This is necessary, not just to raise the quality of verses that do not appear to have any intrinsic literary qualities—we have already been forced by the written situation to exclude many verses which, in the oral context, created much entertainment and enjoyment among the audience—but to encourage the reader to use his imagination to increase his enjoyment and understanding. Indeed it has been generally recognised by scholars of the oral tradition that the only means of successfully conveying the impact of the oral performance would be to use the full range of audio-visual equipment; for example, Ruth Finnegan, *Limba Stories and Story Telling* (Oxford, 1967); 'Introduction', Herskovits & Herskovits, *Dahomean Narrative* (Northwestern 1958); 'Introduction', Ulli Beier, *Yoruba Poetry* (Cambridge, 1970); 'Introduction', G. T. Basden, *Niger Ibos* 1938 (Cass 1966). Not only does one get a more meaningful understanding of the verses by a knowledge of their cultural and ceremonial context; a more imaginative reality derives from seeing and hearing the performers.

Let us take, for example, the Abigbo Song from Mbaise area. The Abigbo group is normally made up of young men between 20 and 40, of no formal education, of independent means through trade in cloths, fish, articles, palm oil and kernels. Their trade makes them spend much time on the road though they travel no great distances by modern standards. As a consequence, they have a measure of emancipation of the mind which derives from travelling, and the independence to say things as they see them, which belongs to those who feel they are fully capable of feeding themselves and their families. And yet, as they return to their locality daily or after trading ventures of a maximum duration of three days, they still have a firm grounding in their values. The result is a robust mentality which appears in the songs in the first instance, but principally in the way the songs are presented to the community.

The performance then is important, both as an accompaniment to the song and even in the very order in which the songs are presented. Abigbo is mainly a dance or dance-play.

This is an aspect of the audience—performer awareness which has other facets. One is the order in which songs are performed. The spirit has to be on the ascendant for certain songs to be performed. On one recording occasion, the group refused to perform one of the most popular satirical songs because the dance 'was not yet properly cooked'; it had not reached the right pitch of excitement which would liberate their spirit and body to perform it right. Their apprehension was justified, for when later it was performed, the audience were completely taken out of themselves and their other thoughts so that they were thoroughly immersed in the mood of the song. Often the progression is from general statement, to public topics, to personal satire. By the time the group arrives at the personal satirical songs the singer/dancers are thoroughly warmed up, and the audience is in a mood of complete excitement; and one is likely to hear reactions like '*O hitiele!*' (it has hit, or it has heated up) and '*akwasa!*'

Another facet of the oral situation is its effect on the nature of the composition. Because the performer is in contact with his audience, he is capable of interjecting

[3]

references to individuals without confusing the audience as to the trend of the main material. He is able to shift from one situation of thought to another, indicating that he is doing so by a mere change of facial expression or gesture of the hand or body. Moreoever, and this is significant, except for narration, the oral situation calls for succinct statements rather than for long logical discussion. The performer is therefore expected to show expertise, not in the building up of a complicated sequence of thought, but in the variety of expressions with which he can state, expand and deepen a single statement. When this fails the result is uninteresting tautology. When it succeeds it is a marvellous exposition of imaginative wealth.

In writing these verses down, therefore, there has been the need to cut out from the transcription those interjected passages which were the outcome of interplay between the performer and individuals in the audience and keep to the main line of thought. Even so, the cumulative rather than the progressive development of the oral performance has had to be preserved so as not to falsify the material. The reader will have to maintain an awareness of this compositional technique to achieve an understanding of some of the verses. The steady syncopated rhythm of the drumming and the abandoned elegance of the dancing constitute an enlargement of the imaginative context of the song.

In addition to various steps, gestures and facial expressions for example, when they sing of the woman who has a lover in every market place, they point towards the four points of the compass, both the pointing and words combining to create the firm impression of the world coverage of the woman's amorous activities. Dancing, and sometimes satirical expressions are often accompanied by the enlargement of the eyes, a tortured twisting of the mouth and the pressing forward of the chest as if to say, 'What can you do to us? We will say what we like!' or the dancers throw up their hands in despair, or in an appeal to God, as an accompaniment to mere sounds and thereby give their meaning.

The rhythmic excitement of traditional songs can only be faintly glimpsed in the versions here. The intricate interplay between voice and drum and dance step demands a high level of expertise which, when achieved, redounds to the glory of the dance group and the excitement of the audience.

(b) *Translation*

The difficulties of attempting to reproduce in translation the literature of another language have been recognized and discussed for a long time. These difficulties assume large proportions when the material is poetry which as Coleridge defined it is 'the best words in the best order'. Having experienced the poems in the text in the oral situation we are even more aware that what we have on the translation pages represents a minimal proportion of the total experience of the original.

In translating therefore, we have tried to keep to a middle road. We have tried to preserve, where it is possible, the original patterns of thought and imagery while not destroying the normal requirements of English expression.

D. I.Nwoga

2. Cultural background Life in Igbo society is full of cultural activities which follow a rhythmical pattern from the womb to the tomb. Each stage of a man's life is marked by one important cultural performance, which turns out a drama of the particular stage.

[5]

Thus at birth we have the names given to the child, which are a wish and blessing, and which dedicate the baby born to the care of the gods. There is also a special ritual which marks the transition from adolescence to adulthood, with utterances of encouragement and vindication. Later in life, one takes one or more of the numerous titles, the occasion of which is one of pomp and self-glorification. Finally, at the time of death, ceremonies follow some cultural pattern. Besides these, there are three cultural features which sometimes accompany them and sometimes stand on their own: namely, religion, magic and festivals. Also moonlight play in which children and adults may take part is an important feature of traditional Igbo society. Each of these cultural activities is accompanied by significant poetic expression, which not only beautifies and records the occasion, but also perpetuates it.

(a)*Naming Ceremony*

The birth of a child, especially a male, is a thing of joy in Igbo society. It is an occasion for merriment among the people and for offering special thanskgiving sacrifices to the family deities. The child is welcomed into the world and dedicated to the gods who will protect and guide him, it is hoped, throughout his life on earth. He is 'brought before the shrines with some offerings', which may be a cock (in the case of a male child), a hen (in the case of a female child), and a goat if the parents can afford it.[1] The parents and relations give the child a series of names, which include doxological statements made to God the creator and praise-names expressing hopes and wishes of success and greatness in life for the child. 'Other names may be given to show the market day on which [the] child was

[1]   Francis A. Arinze, *Sacrifice in Igbo Religion* (Ibadan: Ibadan University Press, 1970), p. 42.

born, or the preference for boys. . . .'[2] Naturally, the names given depend on whether the child is male or female. In the society in general, boys are preferred to girls because it is a boy and not a girl who will continue the family line after the death of the father. The significance and beauty of the names given to a child, male or female, are such as are characteristic of poetry, for in our society poetry importantly deals with life in its past, present and future contexts.

(b) *Puberty Ceremony*

The ceremony that marks the passage from adolescence to adulthood varies from section to section in the society, but the principles, implications and expectations are generally similar. In some places the male ceremony is one of a series of masquerade activities, in which the candidates do a daily race, running after the masquerade through all the villages in the town, and are, besides, subjected to very trying tasks for months. In some other places it may assume the shape of war exercises in which the candidates are rigorously trained in the art of war at the village level. As for girls, the puberty ritual invariably involves confinement, fattening and practice in home management. Whatever shape it takes, for boys the aim is always to prepare them effectively for the precarious life of continuous struggle and endurance which is the lot of man in life, and for girls the objective is to prepare them for mothercraft. The female ceremony normally ends in a wedding, during which wedding songs of well-wishing and expectations are addressed to the candidates.

(c) *Title-Taking Ceremony*

In Igbo society taking a title is a mark of social

[2] Victor Uchendu, *The Igbo of Southeast Nigeria* (New York: Holt, Rinehart and Winston, 1965), p. 60.

[7]

distinction. The titles taken may have different names in different towns and villages, for example, *Ozo* in Udi and *Ndichie* in Onitsha, but the significance is the same. The economic, social and political significance of title-taking is generally remarkable. As Victor Uchendu has correctly observed, the title society is a kind of insurance group which enables the 'socially ambitious to invest the savings he accumulated in his youth while guaranteeing him continued economic support and prestige during his old age. It provides him with a Pan-Igbo passport which he carries with him, a passport which guarantees him all perquisites and accords him a place of honour and dignity among "foreign" associations which would otherwise give him a hostile reception.'[3] One spends a lot of money and other items of wealth to get initiated into the title; and he is in turn qualified for a share of the money and other things provided by all subsequent candidates. It is by this method that he gets dividends on his investment.

It has also been observed that 'in general a man may not, during his father's lifetime, take a title equal to or higher than one held by his father.'[4] This is not true of some parts of Igboland. In Udi Division, for example, it is possible for one to take the *Ozo* title while his father has only the *Ici* title, which is lower in rank. The explanation is that if the father is very old, he considers it unnecessary to embark for himself on the stupendous expenditure involved in the *Ozo* title. Where such a father has the means, he rather elects to finance the title-taking for his son, who, all things being well, has more time than the father to live on earth. In economic terms, such a son will very likely live

[3] *Ibid.*, p. 82.
[4] Daryll Forde and G. I. Jones, *The Ibo and Ibibio Speaking Peoples of Nigeria* (London: International African Institute, 1950), p. 19.

[8]

long enough to harvest from the *Ozo* society more than, or at least as much as, had been invested. Furthermore, where a father has attained the *Ozo* title, it is a mark of special respect for him to finance his son's title-taking. Both instances are in keeping with the traditional prayer of the average Igbo man: that his sons may be greater than or as great as he. And it is all the more glorious and satisfying for him to remain alive and see his prayer materialize.

'Titles are both an expression of wealth and a means of exercising the power it confers.'[5] The social and political status which the title-holders assume is great, for it is sacred. The *Ozo* men, for example, are priests as well as local leaders. 'Titled men ... in the past virtually monopolized authority in their village group. The making of major political decisions and the administration of criminal justice were carried out at public meetings at which all the adult males of the community had a right to express their opinions, and the decisions agreed upon were ratified and virtually imposed by the lineage heads.'[6] In fact, this holds true in some areas at present as in the past.

One who has succeeded in scaling such a social height has, therefore, a feeling of pride and is often intoxicated by the fact of this achievement. The names which he assumes are, therefore, self-praising ones by means of which he rehearses his past experiences and heroic feats, and vindicates his power, majesty and excellence.

(d) *Religion*

The Igbo people are by nature religious. There is hardly any serious life activity in the society which is not very intimately punctuated by a religious exercise

[5] *Ibid.*
[6] *Ibid.*

or expression. The entire life of the people follows a culturally rhythmical pattern marking a cycle from birth to death, in which life begins and ends with religious sacrifices. It is true that their traditional religion is a primitive one but it is also true that their religious spirit is sincere and devoted.

The traditional Igbo religion is one of the forces and elements of nature. There is the 'deification of the sky as a generator of fecundating rain, that of the earth as a fertilized substance producing life, that of many rivers, mountains, various geographical peculiarities . . .', and this type of religion reflects an 'agrarian cult'.[7] Besides the natural forces and phenomena, the dead, that is ancestors, are also worshipped among the Igbo people.

The main gods have spirits who are their servants and agents, intermediaries between them and man. These are the good spirits, who are worshipped as well. The evil spirits are looked upon as the enemies of man, and sacrifices are often offered to the gods and the good spirits so that they may drive them away. It is thus wrong for Maurice Delafosse to say that 'there are not good spirits and bad spirits', and that 'the animism of the Negroes has nothing of dualism and that which has led several missionaries to present it under this aspect can be only a subjective reminiscence of the opposition made by certain Christians between God and the Devil'.[8] In Igbo society just as there are good people and bad people, there are correspondingly good spirits and evil spirits.[9] The prayers of the elders

---

[7]   Maurice Delafosse, *The Negroes of Africa : History and Culture* (Washington: The Associated Publishers, Inc., 1931), p. 219. (cf. G. T. Basden, *Among the Igbos of Nigeria* [London: Frank Cass & Co. Ltd., 1966], p. 217.)

[8]   *Ibid.*, p. 220.

[9]   Cf. Arinze, *op. cit.*, p. 37.

and priests often contain the plea that they be protected from evil men and evil spirits. In fact to the Igbo people there is a notion of correspondence between this world and the land of the dead; and there is not much difference between the world of the living and that of the dead, except that the latter is mysterious and unknown, and the inhabitants all powerful.

This does not mean, however, that the Igbo religion is different from other religions in practice and in purpose. There is still the same set of rites 'invocations, sacrifices, offerings, prayers' and the purpose is always to ask the god to 'accord what is expected of it and keep away what is feared'.[10] The invocations are particularly significant because they summarize the life conditions of the people, their attitudes to life, their relationship with their gods and what they hope will be their relationship with their fellow men.

(e) *Magic and Magicians*

Magic is intimately associated with religion in Igbo society, for it is based on communication with supernatural powers for its functioning and efficacy. Its effects are also similar to those of religion: protection from evil spirits and evil men and success in life ventures. According to Delafosse, 'magic proposes to obtain by the intervention of occult powers of which one becomes the master, that which man, reduced to his own forces, could not procure for himself.'[11] And there is also the same superstitious belief which punctuates the traditional religion. One respect in which our magic differs from our religion is the fact that there is an element of science in one of the functions of the magician, that is, healing or curing. 'By the scientific observer some few of these "medicines"

10 Delafosse, *op. cit.*, pp. 230-231.
11 *Ibid.*, p. 238.

[11]

would be found on investigation to have a biochemical efficiency (e.g. castor oil); while to others, the majority, he would attribute a psychological efficiency.'[12]

It is on the functions of the magicians that Delafosse based his classification of them: exorcists or healers, who expel evil forces; fetishers, who make amulets and talismans; fortune-tellers, who predict the future and discover secrets; spell binders, who cast spells on people and infect them with diseases; and prestidigitators, who conjure by the force of words only.[13] Godfrey Wilson also uses function as a basis for his own classification, but comes up with a different set of types: ceremonial magic, magic of private ambition, sorcery or destructive magic, magic for cure of sickness and trouble, and magic of appeal.[14] All these types do actually exist in Igbo society, but there is just one name for them, that is, *dibia*, which can symbolize a man or a masquerade.

Many people agree that the effect of magic is more psychological than otherwise; and it is by means of words that the magician achieves this effect. This is true of magic in Igbo society; it is equally true of the mystic exercises in other cultures. The power of words in all supernatural communication is an established belief. Even in the sacrifice of the Mass, Catholics believe that 'Transubstantiation' is effected as the celebrant pronounces the words of Consecration. Such words, incantations, used by the Igbo magicians are believed to be powerful and efficacious. It is, therefore, surprising that Wilson had to remark that 'in most

---

[12] Godfrey Wilson, 'An African Morality,' in *Cultures and Societies of Africa*, eds. Simon and Phoebe Ottenberg (New York: Random House, 1960), p. 359.

[13] Delafosse, *op. cit.*, p. 237.

[14] Wilson, *op. cit.*, p. 359.

magical rituals', that is, in Nyakyusa, East Africa, 'words are not an essential factor at all; to some few, however, they are integral'.[15] One is tempted to think that if this was what Wilson actually observed, then Nyakyusa must be a terrible exception, not only in Africa, but also in the whole sphere of magical or mystical operations.

(f) *Festivals*

Festivals are so many and varied in Igbo society that one need only comment on the major ones. Even what G. T. Basden regards as 'fixed festivals'[16] differ from place to place in the society, though *Ifejoku*, that is, harvest festival, is fairly common. Also masquerade festivals are common among the people of Udi and Nsukka, the *Odo* masquerade festival being the most popular.

The festival period, irrespective of the type it happens to be, is often one of relaxation, enjoyment and worship. The reason for sacrificing during the festival depends on when it features. If the feast is one marking the beginning of the harvest season, people offer sacrifices to their deity to thank him for keeping them and their families alive to see another season of plenty. If on the other hand it is a festival marking the beginning of a planting season, people pray to their gods for health and strength to be able to do their farm work effectively, and ask them to ward off antagonistic spirits from their farms and homes. After harvests, people also celebrate and offer sacrifices to the gods and offer them the biggest yams or other crops from their farms. This is done in appreciation of the gods' care, guidance and protection.

[15] *Ibid.*
[16] G. T. Basden, *Among the Ibos of Nigeria* (London: Frank Cass & Co. Ltd., 1966), p. 227.

[13]

It is during this third kind of festival and the masquerade festival that people have the longest period of relaxation. The whole period is often one of eating, drinking, singing and dancing. If it happens to be, and sometimes it is, when there is a full moon, the singing and dancing often assume the shape of a moonlight play.

(g) *Moonlight Play*

In the past, the moonlight play was such an important cultural feature that it drew adults as well as children to the *Oboli* or *Mbala* (village square) for singing, dancing, reciting of riddles, tongue-twisters and jocular and satirical poems. But with the intrusion of 'civilization' and the tendency of most of the capable and skilled adults to seek employment in urban centres, this aspect of Igbo culture is more and more the concern of children. Even then, many children do not any longer attend the play because they are in schools away from their homes. However, the cultural significance of the moonlight play still exists even if the practice of it has diminished.

One vital aspect of the play is its atmosphere of freedom. The singers are free to satirize social malpractices irrespective of the personages involved; obscene references are made where the need arises; children who are otherwise shy and retreating come out of their shells and for once exercise their power of expression. The more sex-inclined adults find some dark corners and engage in their fleshly game. The fact that the moonlight play is rather occasional limits its chances for encouraging irresponsibility, while it is to its credit that it provides a free atmosphere for expression and for learning the art of story telling and poetry reciting.

(h) *Funeral Ceremonies*

A funeral ceremony in Igbo society involves sacrifices, singing and dancing. According to the traditional concept, the end of a man's journey through life is remarkable because it is a stage at which the gods have decided to claim back what they gave to the world. It is much more so if the dead person is a title holder, or has otherwise distinguished himself in a spectacular way in the society. To mark this important point in time of a man's history, some ceremonies are carried out.

Religious sacrifice is one of such ceremonies, and the sacrifice is offered for a number of reasons. According to Rev. Arinze, such sacrifices 'are made to the ancestors to ask them to accept the spirit of the deceased into their company, to overlook any of his past misdeeds, and to show the ancestors that the living had good relations with the deceased and had nothing against his future happiness. Some sacrifices are offered to the non-human spirits with shrines to pay them what the deceased might have owed them. The dead man's *Chi* [personal god], family and village spirits ... receive special attention. The chief motive seems to be that they may facilitate matters for the deceased.'[17]

Though this observation has taken into account most of the reasons for offering sacrifices at funerals, it has left out one important point. This is the fact that most of the sacrifices are offered primarily to the spirit of the deceased himself so that he would have some provision to carry him through the journey to the land of the dead. This explains why in some cases the title holder is buried with a ram and a cock hung round his neck. It is generally believed in all cases that if the sacrificial rites are not performed, the deceased will keep hanging

[17]   Arinze, *op. cit.*, p. 41.

about between this world and the other world and cannot reach the land of the dead until those rites are performed.

The other features of a funeral ceremony are singing, dancing and firing of guns. Women do the singing in which they praise the deceased, blame death for taking him away, lament the loss, and occasionally satirize the living. The dancing is done by the elders and members of the age group of the deceased, with the music supplied by the *Ikpa* and *Igede* drummers. It is a farewell ritual performed exclusively to honour the dead man. Guns are fired by the young men to bid the deceased goodbye and to let the towns around know of the departure of an important man. When all these things have been done, it is believed that the deceased reaches the land of the dead peacefully and joyfully. There is no possibility of his hanging about on the way or appearing in this world in broad daylight to frighten and harass people, especially his relations.

R. N. Egudu

1 PRAISE POEMS

translated by R. N. Egudu

PRAISE OF AN **INFLUENTIAL** **MAN**	The son of Ezenovo's son of the line of hill movers, The brother of the *Ozo*, son of the hard Iron-King The brother of the *Ozo*, who is the Knife that cuts bushes, The son of Amadiwhe, who is the King that cuts through hills, The brother of the *Ozo*, who eats accompanied with the music of the gong, Shall I praise you once or twice? By the right or by the left? See him—one who though short is not a dwarf For shortness is the natural compression of effect.

PRAISE OF AN **ARTIST-SINGER**	Call for me that human child, who invokes the *Odo*, The son of the man, who is Strength that condemns cowardice, The son of the King, who is called *Iva*, The lively child, who knew how to invoke the *Odo* When the going was good, The human that invokes Spirits, Would you intone your chant, The human that invokes Spirits, Son of Strength-that-condemns-cowardice, Call for me Those who 'eat' with me the *Odo* songs, Call for me Those with whom I have always fought on war-hills.

PRAISE OF AN **OZO TITLE** **HOLDER**	*Ozo*, fulfilled in the cult of *Ozo*, *Ozo*, the blower of the *Ozala*,[1] *Ozo*, king, who is the Sun-tree,

[1] Musical flute made from the tusk of an elephant.

Son of 'Two Giant Ants' with eight feathers,
Son of 'One Palm-Nut' which yields oil that fills
   a pot,
Dried pepper that does not fill the gourd
But is very hot;
Call for me the one who took the *Ozo* title as a
   youth,
The King, who is the Crest of the Hill,
The Chief who is the High Priest of Hills and
   Valleys,
Master of the spiritual craftsmanship.

PRAISE OF A HERO

Young man, you are:
A hare that ascends a hill running
A rope that drags the elephant along
A lion that kills the tiger
A head that never touches the ground
A log of the *inyi*[1] wood

PRAISE OF A BEAUTIFUL LADY

Young lady, you are:
A mirror[2] that must not go out in the sun
A child that must not be touched by dew
One that is dressed up in hair
A lamp with which people find their way
Moon that shines bright
An eagle feather[2] worn by a husband
A straight line drawn by God.

[1] The inyi tree is regarded as the hardest tree, and a log of it
as the hardest and heaviest log.
[2] The mirror and the eagle-feather are symbols of beauty and
nobility respectively.

OZO TITLE HOLDER PRAISING HIMSELF:

(a) BASED ON FARMING

I am:
One who tills hills
One who with yams challenges soil
Knife that clears bushes
Barn that is wide
Bush that yields wealth
Bush that is colossal
Bush that is fearful
Hoe-User untouched by hunger.

(b) BASED ON WINE TAPPING

I am:
Height that is fruitful
Climbing rope that makes king
Knife that harvests money
Wealth from height.

(c) BASED ON HUNTING

I am:
Killer of tiger
Tiger that roams in wilderness
Bullet that gives life
Tiger with claws
King of wilderness.

(d) BASED ON TRADING

I am:
Awho-market that is greater than *Ubulu*-market
Nkwo-market that is fruitful
Nkwo-market that carries wealth
Eke-market that is admirable
Elephant that carries wealth
Vehicle that carries wealth.

[21]

I am:
One whose father is elephant
One whose father gave him eagle-feather
Brotherhood that is mysterious
Heir grateful to father
One to whom personal god gave eagle-feather
One who is never tired of making money
King accepted by neighbours. ....

('Elephant' is a symbol of opulence, dignity and renown. It is taken to be the king of animals. In the same way, the *Ozo* regards his own father as the king of men for having provided him with the right to take the title and the money for footing the bill.

'Eagle-feather' is a symbol of glory and nobility. As the eagle is regarded as the noble king of birds, so is the *Ozo* regarded as the glorious, noble king of his community. Every *Ozo* man therefore wears an eagle-feather on the right hand side of his hat.

'Brotherhood that is mysterious' is a negative name. It implies that the *Ozo* was not assisted by his brothers when he took the title. That is to say, although other people may think that his brothers were brotherly to him, yet behind the façade of consanguinity, it was all hatred and lack of cooperation among them.

The last line is an uncompleted name.

The idea is that if one is accepted as a king by his immediate circle, outsiders will naturally accept him as such.)

I am:
Tiger that defends neighbours
King that is liked by public
Fame that never wanes
Flood that can't be impeded
Ocean that can't be exhausted
Wealth that gives wisdom

[22]

Child with washed hands. . . .
Child that accomplished a difficult journey
    quickly. . . .[1]

(g) **BASED ON**   I am:
    PHYSICAL   King to be admired
    BEAUTY   King of beauty
            King son of Eagle[2]
            King of Sunshine[2]
            Eagle of community
            Mirror[2] for neighbours.

        ODO   May the congregation here listen,
MASQUERADER   Listen
   PRAISING   For it's the *Odo* that hears the market din
   HIMSELF   The *Odo* that lives near the *Nkwo*-market,
            Speaking his mind—his eternal mind:
            I say to you,

[1]   The last two lines are often left hanging, but people gener-
ally know the complement. The full ideas conveyed by the
lines are as follows:
    (a) A child who has washed his hands clean should sit at
       table with the adults.
       The *Ozo* in this context looks upon himself as a child
       who has attained the status of those much older than
       he is.
    (b) A child that accomplishes a difficult journey more
       quickly than normal is often regarded as a prodigy;
       and people say that he operates under a supernatural
       influence. Similarly those who do not particularly
       like the man who has taken the *Ozo* title much earlier
       than expected often allege that he got money by some
       supernatural means.

[2]   'Eagle', 'sunshine' and 'mirror' are all symbols of beauty.

[23]

No other *Odo* gnaws into my trunk
And into my branches
Except the one of Ugwu-Odegbulu line,
Okpoko[1]
Who thundered and ate his visitor;
I am the *Odo* who feeds on the market din—
I *Ogene* the bell for calling conferences,
I, the beaked-singer that rips open the maize-cub,
I, the mysterious tripod used for cooking
So that the pot can stand erect,
Two of my three legs give way
And the pot falls off, rolling
Seeking the eternal cook.

I ask the creator-scatterer of locusts
To please retreat a pace
For Almighty *Odo* son of Diuyoko is girded with
    cloth
And is going in peace—
If soldier ants advance, one advances,
If they retreat, one retreats;
He who has a basket should bring it to the
    wilderness
For the numberless locusts
Are hovering in a host in the wilderness.

I, the *Ozo* who killed an elephant
I, the *Ozo* who wore palm-leaves and rejected the
    hoe,
I, the *Ozo*, who took his title on *Eke* day
And displayed at the village square on *Olie* day;
I, the beaked-Singer
I, the thorny weed never used as a carrying pad;
I, the branch of the Iyi-tree that becomes a medicine –
The killer of other trees—

[1] Hornbill.

[24]

I am the wood-pecker
That destroys trees,
The tree we consecrated
Has ever been my walking-stick—
 Ha—Ha—Ha—Ha—

I am the *Odo* that flew straight and touched the
 whole Igboland
The *Odo* living in the square of the King of
 Contentment
The *Odo*, whose gate is the *Ngwu* tree;
I am like the child who did a hard journey fast
And was said to have raced under supernatural
 influence
I am the craftsman of the spirit world.

I am a gong:
The gong is inspired
And it begins to talk:
I am the gong with a melodious voice,
The crowd is thick here,
The white ants are fluttering
They are in clusters;
My *uturu*-voice[1]
nightingale.
Is singing in the *Odo*-fashion;
I've come, I've come, I've come,
Son of the Almighty *Odo*:
The copyist cannot pick up
All that flows from my voice, what I am singing,
I, the *Uturu*.

| MALE NAMES | Oke-Cukwu | God's creation |
| | Ike-Cukwu | Strength of God |

[1] *Uturu* is a bird noted for singing; it is the equivalent of the
 nightingale.

[25]

Cukwu-dị	God exists
Cukwu-ka	God is supreme
Cukwu-kelu	God did the creation
Cukwu-emeka	God has done well
Chi-bụ-eze	God is king
Eze-Cukwu	A king from God
Eze-akọ	A king is never lacking
Eze-di-nma	A king that is beautiful
Eze-bụ-chi	A king is God
Madụ-bụ-ọghụ	A person is a joy
Madụ-ka-akụ	A person is greater than wealth
Madụ-bụ-chi	A person is God
Madụ-bụ-ike	A person is strength
Okawhọ	Male born on Awhọ day
Okonkwọ	Male born on Nkwo day
Okeke	Male born on Eke day
Okolie	Male born on Olie day

FEMALE NAMES	Ada-nma	Queen of beauty
	Ngwa-nma	Sign of beauty
	Ezi-nma	Real beauty
	Ugo-di	Eagle of husband
	Ugo-nna	Eagle of father
	Ugo-ọha	Eagle of people
	Akụ-nna	Wealth of father
	Akụ-Cukwu	Wealth from God
	Ụnọ-dị-akụ	House of wealth
	Nwa-ka-akụ	Child is greater than wealth
	Ụzọ-akụ	Road to wealth
	Ngọzị-Cukwu	Blessing from God
	Ngọzị-ka	Blessing is supreme
	Ụzọ-ego	Road to money
	Nwa-ka-ego	Child is greater than money
	Chi-ọma	Luck from God
	Ije-ọma	Journey to luck

Ihe-ọma	Gift of luck
Chi-nyelụ	Gift from God
Chi-nwe	Property of God

PUBERTY PRAISE SONG (for a Female): MONEY

She was married with money
    Money   (Chorus)
One like her husband
    Money
Fertile egg
    Money
Eagle of surplus beauty
    Money
Husband's sweetheart
    Money
Breast that feeds a child
    Money
Conduct that is highest valued
    Money
Woman is the joy of a home
    Money.

SHE HAS RETURNED TO HIS HOUSE

She has returned, she has returned to his house
  (Chorus)
    The beautiful child
She has returned, she has returned to his house
    The great child
She has returned, she has returned to his house
    The well-behaved child
She has returned, she has returned to his house
    To the house of a rich man
She has returned, she has returned to his house.

ADMIRE BEAUTY   Admire the queen of beauty
         Admire   (Chorus)
Admire the fruit of beauty
         Admire
Admire the eagle-like beauty
         Admire
Admire the lady of beauty
         Admire

UMBRELLA   An umbrella is held over the beautiful child
      Iya — Iya — Iya   (Chorus)
The beautiful one is returning home
      Iya — Iya — Iya
An umbrella is held over the beautiful thing
      Iya — Iya — Iya
A beautiful thing has happened
      Iya — Iya — Iya

2 INVOCATION POEMS

translated by R. N. Egudu

PROTECTION   My God and ancestors
I thank you
For letting me see this day;
May I continue to see more
Till my hair becomes white;
May the hoe never cut my feet;
Protect me and my household
From evil men and spirits;
I wish no man evil,
But if anyone says I have lived too long,
Let him go before me to see
What it is like in the land of the dead;
The man who holds on to *ǫwhǫ*[1]
Cannot get lost in his journey.

KOLA-NUT   Hills, take kola-nut
Earth, take kola-nut
Sun, take kola-nut
Valleys, take kola-nut
Ancestors, take kola-nut:
Go before us
Stand behind us
We don't eat kola-nut with its radicle[2]
We eat what is due to humans
We don't eat what is due to Spirits:
Take, all of you, your kola radicle
Take, all of you, the slices of kola-nut
ISE-E............*ISE-E*[3]   (Chorus)

LIFE   God the Creator,
Sky and Earth,

[1]   A sacred staff which symbolizes righteousness.
[2]   The radicle belongs to the deities as of right.
[3]   The equivalent of 'Amen'.

[31]

Sun of the Supreme Creator,
Our Ancestors:
It is life
And what it is supported with—
Wealth upon wealth —
These we ask of you.

3 INCANTATION POEMS

translated by R. N. Egudu

CAUTION If a man taps palm wine and cooks food,
One or the other is fated to be badly done;
The man who stands firm by his falsehood
Is more dignified than he who deserts his truth;
Frequenting the fortune teller's shrine
Does not always bring one wisdom;
A dog is deep in thought
And is thought to be asleep;
A tortoise is advised to be ready for a foe,
But he is already lying in ambush;
One who pursues a den to its end
Often ends up losing his fingers;
The pursuer after the innocent fowl
Is doomed to fall down;
The stick used for removing a millipede
Is often thrown away with it;
One who has not eaten the *udala* fruit
Never suffers from the disease caused by it;
For one who holds on to *ọwhọ*
Is never lost in a journey

SPIRIT POT Spirit pot;
It is filled and unfilled at once!
One who hurries into a fight
Does not realize that to fight is to die!
One who has broken the *inyi* wood,
Can the *akpaka* wood defy him?
A worn-out basket:
It is recovered for use on the day of sacrifice!
If the vultures were meant to be eaten as food
The ancestors would have exhausted them!
Magic paraphernalia:
They are never lacking in a *Dibia*'s[1] bag!

[1] A magician or herbalist.

[35]

If the sky-vulture looms,
The devil enters the eagle's eye!

WHAT WILL IT BE? What will it be today?
Success or failure?
Death or life?
Ha! the flood cannot run up the hill.
What is this evil spirit that throws his shade
Between me and the truth?
I hold my sacred staff against it.
Here is the east, there is the west;
Here the sun rises—
See the truth come riding on the rays of the sun.
The Sky and the Earth keep me company,
And can my tongue go zig-zag?[1]
The grey hair is an enemy of lies.
Come, the spirits of my forefathers,
Stand by your son.
Let us show this client of ours what we can do
We have been known for this power:
If one cuts the *Ngwu* tree by noon,
It mocks him with a new shoot before the sun
    falls[2]
Speak, speak to your son.

INVINCIBLE Market is higgle-haggle;
If the market meets not, the pot cooks not,
Fowl never confers with fox;
Heavy she-goat is above being dragged;
White goat never confers with wolf;
Butterfly never sinks in a pit;

[1] Can I tell lies?
[2] Before sunset.

Empty calabash never sinks in water;
Basket never collects water;
Stone never answers a call;
Back of palm picks nothing from the ground;
Fight for peace never eats a hero;
The evil one causes stays put with him;
Blabbing made shrew's mouth pointed;
Smoke goes first, and fire follows.

4 DANCE POEM: IGODO

translated by R. N. Egudu

We've come to sing *Igodo*
      d: d: d: d: d: s: d:——[1]
Sons of *Odo* living near*Ngwu* tree
Do the dance with your feet
But who is it who is saying it?
But who is it who is singing it?
It's the son of *Odo* living near*Ngwu* tree
Odo living near Nkwo market is saying it
But what is it done with?
Beef and pork.

Ozo fulfilled as *Ozo*
Ozo of *Ngwu* town
Killer of famous Ram
Ram's hair is its fame
Ram's horn is its strength
Killer of famous Ram
But what do you do it with?
Where is your musical horn?
Where is your cow-head?
Where is your pig-head?
Blow the musical horn
Odo by*Nkwo* market inspires you
Four-headed *Odo* inspires you
Odo by*Ngwu* tree inspires you
Blow the musical horn
Let our Earth take *ọwhọ*
Take *ọwhọ* and pray
Let our Hills[2] take *ọwhọ*
Take *ọwhọ* and pray
A Hill is never a valley
Take *ọwhọ* and pray
Ọwhọ is our weapon

[1] This is hummed by the chorus after every line.
[2] Idols.

One holding on to *ǫwhǫ* is never lost
One holding on to *ǫwhǫ* possesses truth
One holding on to *ǫwhǫ* lacks nothing
Sun is watching
Heaven and Earth are watching

Chorus-singers
Beat the gong with your hand
Do the dance with your feet
Where are my chorus-singers?
Sing me *Igodo* song
Who is it who is saying it?
I am the one saying it
I, son of *Odo* living near *Ngwu* tree
I, son of *Odo* living near *Nkwo* market
I, *uturu*, am singing
I with voice better than musical-horn
My voice is gong's voice
Let my chorus-singers respond
Sons of Almighty Odo
My band of singers
My band of sojourners
We salute owners of the land—
Ozo-men fulfilled nine times nine—
I am the one saying it
I, spokesman for the rest
It is me saying it
I, son of *Odo* living near *Nkwo* market
It is *Odo* who is saying it
Almighty *Odo* is saying it
Sons of Almighty *Odo*
We are celebrating *Igodo*
We are singing *Igodo*
We are drumming *Igodo*
We are dancing *Igodo*
Cock has crowed (about 4.30 a.m.)

Bush fowl has chanted
He who visits has to depart
We have to fly off (i.e. have to disperse)
May you not stumble
Our Hill escort you (i.e. god)
Our Earth escort you (i.e. goddess)
Our *Odo* guard you
Guard your relations
While you adhere to rite of *ọwhọ*

5 RELAXATION POEMS

translated by R. N. Egudu

BREAD FRUIT
What happened to Nweke Njeghiliọna?
   (name of a person)
E—E Nweke Njeghiliọna;
Bread-fruit crushed Nweke Njeghiliọna
E—E Nweke Njeghiliọna.

What happened to Bread-fruit?
Splinter split bread-fruit
Bread-fruit crushed Nweke Njeghiliọna,
E—E Nweke Njeghiliọna.

What happened to splinter?
Fire burnt splinter
Splinter split bread-fruit
Bread-fruit crushed Nweke Njeghiliọna,
E—E Nweke Njeghiliọna.

What happened to fire?
Water quenched fire
Fire burnt splinter
Splinter split bread-fruit
Bread-fruit crushed Nweke Njeghiliọna,
E—E Nweke Njeghiliọna.

What happened to water?
Goat drank water
Water quenched fire
Fire burnt splinter
Splinter split bread-fruit
Bread-fruit crushed Nweke Njeghiliọna,
E—E Nweke Njeghiliọna.

What happened to goat?
Death killed goat
Goat drank water
Water quenched fire

[47]

Fire burnt splinter
Splinter split bread-fruit
Bread-fruit crushed Nweke Njeghiliọna,
E—E Nweke Njeghiliọna.

Who created death?
God created death
Death killed goat
Goat drank water
Water quenched fire
Fire burnt splinter
Splinter split bread-fruit
Bread-fruit crushed Nweke Njeghiliọna,
E—E Nweke Njeghiliọna.

MISSING RAT

Child was looking for his rat
    Nda
His rat was lying in tiger's house
    Nda
Tiger's house was by the road to all tigers
    Nda

Brother was looking for his brother
    Nda
His brother was looking for his rat
    Nda
His rat was lying in tiger's house
    Nda
Tiger's house was by the road to all tigers
    Nda

Mother was looking for her son
    Nda
Her son was looking for his brother
    Nda

[48]

His brother was looking for his rat
Nda
His rat was lying in tiger's house
Nda
Tiger's house was by the road to all tigers
Nda

Father was looking for his wife
Nda
His wife was looking for her son
Nda
Her son was looking for his brother
Nda
His brother was looking for his rat
Nda
His rat was lying in tiger's house
Nda
Tiger's house was by the road to all tigers
Nda

SHREW My brother
Nda
My brother
Nda
Your trap has caught game
Nda
What has it caught?
Nda
It has caught a shrew
Nda
Go, take and eat it
Nda
For I won't eat it
Nda
My God, my God
Nda

[49]

Go, take and eat it
Nda
For I won't eat it
Nda

PEAR Give me pear
Parrot's pear,
Give me parrot
Wren's parrot,
Give me wren
Moth's wren,
Give me moth
Palm-tree's moth
Give me palm-tree
Earth's palm-tree,
Give me earth
Earth that yields wealth
Give me wealth
Wealth makes enemies.

CROOKED BUSH I entered a crooked bush
Cut a crooked stick
And staked with it a crooked yam,
Took a crooked digger
And dug out the crooked yam
Gave it to a crooked woman
To cook it on a crooked tripod
It was to be given to a crooked man,
Who then ate the crooked yam.

CROPS Woman who eats beans:
If you eat beans
You must cultivate beans.
And maintain your beans.

[50]

Man who eats cocoyam:
If you eat coco-yam
You must cultivate cocoyam
And maintain your cocoyam.

Child who eats maize:
If you eat maize
You must cultivate maize
And maintain your maize.

Town that eats ground-pea:
If you eat ground-pea
You must cultivate ground-pea
And maintain your ground-pea.

6 SATIRICAL POEMS

*translated by R. N. Egudu
and D. I. Nwoga*

COOKING WOMAN When woman cooks, cooks and the food is never
   done
When woman cooks, cooks and the food is never
   done
Die-hard caller stays, stays, without going:
     Yes Yes Yes, without going
     Yes Yes Yes, without going
Die-hard caller stays, stays, without going.

When woman fries, fries without ending
When woman fries, fries without ending
Die-hard caller stays, stays, without going:
     Yes Yes Yes, without going
     Yes Yes Yes, without going
Die-hard caller stays, stays, without going.

When woman pounds, pounds without finishing
When woman pounds, pounds without finishing
Die-hard caller stays, stays, without going:
     Yes Yes Yes, without going
     Yes Yes Yes, without going
Die-hard caller stays, stays, without going.

YOU! You!
Your head is like a drum that is beaten for spirits.
You!
Your eyes are like balls of fire.
You!
Your ears are like the fans used for blowing fire.
You!
Your nostril is like a mouse's den.
You!
Your mouth is like a mound of mud.
You!
Your hands are like drum-sticks.

[55]

You!
Your belly is like a pot of rotten water.
You!
Your legs are like stakes.
You!
Your buttocks are like a mountain top.

SPINSTER   When I was a Spinster
One young man said he would marry me.
When I reached his house
He explained how the world was with him.
My village companions, do not have fear
I am coming home again.
Young women, my companions
Just go on dancing, the dance is to my taste.

OPEN THE   Open the door for me!
DOOR [1]   Who is it?
Who is it?
I am a young girl from Umuode.
I carry no enmity in my heart.
Who is it?
Who is it?

MEN AGAINST   How a woman calls her husband
WOMEN   When he brings home meat:
(a)   'Look, my master is coming home'
If she looks in his bag
And sees nothing in it

[1]   (From the story of a girl put in the family way by a relief
worker. The man is afraid to admit the girl as she comes
packing back to him.)

'What ill fortune,
I remember the man who should have married
  me.'

(b) We are four from our mother's womb
Three are women and one man;
The women have now gone to husbands' homes
Who now will be my companion?
If I have some trouble
Who will save me, who will save me?
He who has only sisters is a lone child.

WOMEN
AGAINST MEN
(a)

When the world goes hard with men
Men drift and drift along the road
When the world goes hard with women
They pound and pound beside their hearths
I am well off! I am well off!
To be well off:
Is it by boasting or getting rich?

(b) I was going on my way
When the tail of my eye caught my husband
Walking hand in hand with a girl
I asked my husband 'What is this for?'
He said 'Shut up, close your mouth
She is my servant'
Umu chi la edu uwa[1]
That she was his servant
I told my mother-in-law that one of these days
The servant was going to be a wife.
The servant was going to be a wife
So that the little farm there is cut in two,

[1] The praise name of the dance group to whom the story is being told. Literally 'Those whose world is directed by God', i.e. things are all right with them.

The few palm trees are divided into two.
So then I rushed off to the Centre
To the Headmaster's house
There was the house of the Headmaster
Our master, the Headmaster, said, 'daughter do
    not cry,'
That he was going to give him Penance
That a married man
Had no right to two wives
That it was a law of the church.

(c) He is eating in a hotel.[1]
A young man
Is eating in a hotel.
He finished his hotel food
And stole a piece of meat,
He has now gone to prison and
I have laughed myself to pain.

BROTHER-IN-LAW   Brother-in-law that harvested tall palm trees for me,
My husband is angry
Suspecting you are now my lover
Since you say nothing and don't open your mouth
I doubt whether you have your strength
Get up and take me home
A full-grown man now just stares at the world
He now just makes mouth at the world.

WIFE OF OKPEKAỌGỤ   She that cooks and distributes to the public, wife
    of Okpekaọgụ
Why is it you have sent Okpekaọgụ to prison?

[1]   Eating in a hotel is a sign of irresponsibility, and wasteful-
ness. A responsible young man should eat in his house.

[58]

Is it that Okpekaọgụ has no money?
Is it that Okpekaọgụ has no mouth?
What hardens your heart?
Is it because of Sylvester, son of the soil, that your
    heart is hardened?
Having a lover within the kindred is bad,
Having a lover within the kindred is bad,
Okpekaọgụ has gone to prison because his wife had
    a lover within the kindred
Alas! Okpekaọgụ cried,
I am going to Owerri.[1]
As I have no kindred and no brothers
I am gone.

PASSING SIX   *Nye nwelele a —Nye nwelele a —*
NWA   I will to go Obinigwe to buy abortion medicine to
OBINIGWE   eat
    I will to go Obinigwe where 'Passing Six' girls
        nurse babies
    Please Father forgive me for it just happened that
        way to me
    Please Father forgive me for I didn't know I was
        pregnant.

> Why hide your chest, are you a hen?[2]
> Your body did make awful sounds
> *Oghirigho Oghirigho Oghirigho e*
> Hurry down, hurry down and kiss

First Friday girl, the Priest will not forgive you
Legion of Mary girl, the Priest will not forgive you

[1]   The town where the prison is situated.
[2]   The pregnant girl walks bending forward to hide the pro-
jection of her stomach and so is considered to be hiding
her chest.

[59]

Morning Mass girl, the Priest will not forgive you
Because you did it and then bought abortion
    medicine and ate
Because you did it and then bought abortion
    medicine and ate.

PROSTITUTION   All give me your ears
My case needs not much talking
Too much talking is not good
I have come from a distant place
It is notorious, it is not good at all.

Where is Udumma?
It is said she has gone prostituting
Prostituting is not good
It is notorious, it is not good at all.

She caught gonorrhoea[1]
Said she was poisoned
It is notorious, it is not good at all.

I gave my case into the hands of the chiefs
They didn't hear the case, did not discuss it
But said I was guilty
Let peace not be my undoing
It is notorious, it is not good at all.

Where is Udumma?
Her mother was pining away for her
Nothing was said, nothing was discussed
She went off prostituting
Let peace not be my undoing
It is notorious, it is not good at all.

[1]   Literally 'the waist of a monkey'

She became pregnant
Refused to have the baby
Let kindness not be God's undoing
It is notorious, it is not good at all.

She has killed children
That would have come to life
Let kindness not be God's undoing
It is notorious, it is not good at all.

Everyone should avoid Udumma
Her case is over
Let kindness not be God's undoing
It is notorious, it is not good at all.

All give me your ears
Give me your ears
My case needs not too much talking
Too much talking is not good
It is notorious, it is not good at all.

MONICA I was on my way when a pretty boy saw me and
nodded his head
I was on my way when a pretty boy saw me and
nodded his head
He said, 'Hey you girl, come here, come here'
I said, 'Hey you boy, I am on a message, I am on
a message'
I was just by myself when he said to come to his
house
I was just by myself when he said to come to his
house
I had no idea he was upstairs making love to
Monica
I had no idea he was upstairs making love to
Monica

[61]

He touched my head, touched my arms
Touched my eyes, touched my ears
He touched my waist, touched my breasts
He touched my belly, touched my nose
He said, 'Oh baby, do please touch me back'
He said, 'Oh baby, do please touch me back'
He gave me bread to eat and give my consent, No!
He gave me nylon pants to wear and give my
    consent, No!
He bought me chewing gum to eat and give my
    consent, No!
He bought me sweet chim-chim to eat and give my
    consent, No!
He gave me hot kissing to change my mind to
    agree, No!
He touched my waist to change my mind to agree,
    No!
He touched my breasts to change my mind to
    agree, No!
I had no idea he was upstairs making love to
    Monica
Her mother had told her
Monica my daughter
Do not spoil yourself
Today's young men are dancing ajasco[1] on the bed
I had no idea he was upstairs making love to
    Monica
Gbam gbam, Onitsha sector, she'd open, she'd close
Gbam gbam, Okigwe sector, she'd open, she'd close
Gbam gbam, Abagana sector she'd open, she'd close
Monica my daughter, she became pregnant
She became pregnant, she might die of it

[1] Slang name for a jig-like form of dancing made popular by
T.V. It has the connotation of a ruffian dance, and so the
expression means 'Today's young men are making love
recklessly'.

She became pregnant, and wanted to remove it
    but it refused
She was fearful, for her mother had told her
Monica my daughter
Do not spoil yourself
Today's young men dance ajasco on the bed
An event of caution has taken place among us
    young women
A shameful thing has happened among us young
    women
From today all should take care of themselves
Do not be like Monica
If you keep yourself you will marry a good husband
Gbam gbam, Onitsha sector, she'd open and she'd
    close
Gbam gbam, Okigwe sector, she'd open and she'd
    close
Gbam gbam, Abagana sector, she'd open and she'd
    close

JOSEPH   Joseph, Joseph
Joseph, sheep-stealing has exposed you to disgrace
Don't ask me not to tell, for I will tell
Don't ask me not to talk, for I will talk
Joseph, come out and meet your company.[1]
Your mother was rich, your father was rich, you
    must also be rich.
Rather than this why didn't you go kernel-
    gathering?[2]

[1]   This implies that Joseph would now be too ashamed to
meet his mates.

[2]   'Kernel-gathering' is the lowest income-yielding occupation
and is normally the only avenue for poor orphans to earn
their living in folk tales.

[63]

Whatever you do your sopido now[1] disgusts me
You are gathering snails to eat but you are already
    exposed.
Joseph, Joseph
I am just and innocent, God knows, I'm leaving
    you
Joseph, Joseph

MARITTA If you want some fun jump the fence to Maritta
OFOKA   Ofoka
        War!
     Sorry, my lady,[2] go find who put you in your state,
        war!
     My lady, my white sophisticated lady, war!
     Go find who put you in your state, war!
     You, quick to abort, will a basket of pepper serve
        your needs?
        War!
     Sorry, my lady, go find who put you in your state,
        war!
     If you approach Maritta's bed, the stench of
        pomades suffocates you
        war!
     Sorry, my lady, go find who put you in your state,
        war!
     If you get to the lady's bed, her body is playing
        Bongo, war![3]

[1] 'Sopido' was the name of popular shoes for slick young
     men, which had heavy crepe soles that made delightful
     sounds.
[2] This is a free translation of '*oyiwe*' (*oyibo* in other dialects),
     which literally is 'white man or woman' but is used sar-
     castically to designate anybody who behaves in a manner
     aping the whiteman.
[3] Bongo is a new popular dance of young men and women.
     The statement being made is erotic, vulgar.

Sorry, my lady, go find who put you in your state,
war!
When a young girl marries she says her mates are
left-overs,
Sorry, my lady, go find who put you in your state,
war!
He who is displeased will be covered with
kwashiokor,
Sorry, my lady, go find who put you in your state,
war!
She should have known the body was wealth and
was using hers for playing Bongo
Sorry, my lady, go find who put you in your state,
war!
Will I be like Agnes who followed soldiers home?
war!
Sorry, my lady, go find who put you in your state,
war!
Will I be like Eveline who followed soldiers home?
war!
Three sisters who followed soldiers home, war!
Will I, because of rice and beans, get killed by jet
fighters? war!
Sorry, my lady, go find who put you in your state,
war!
Her mother was dying and she went playing Bongo
around the town
In, in, out, out, that is on a girl's body, war!
Supirikiti nnyom, that's the sound from a girl's
body, war!
Maritta Ofoka, go find who put you in your state,
war!

OKAFO The fair man dazzling in the wilderness, Okafo
EZEDIGBO Ezedigbo

[65]

You who introduced meat to the vulture's mouth
    with one hand,
While at the same time introducing faeces with the
    other!
You who threw away a child's bow and helped him
    search for it, Okafo Ezedigbo!
Nwokafo, rise, let us talk, let me tell you what
    I've come for.

DID YOU TELL   When I was cooking sardine for you, did you tell
YOUR MOTHER?   your mother?
My friend Georgina, have patience, oh.
The day I was cooking rice for you, did you tell
    your mother?
Now that you are expecting, you are telling your
    mother
Are you telling her to do what?
To do what? To kill the baby?
If the law catches her, what can you do for her?
Georgina take the *coarse loincloth* and tie, for it now
    suits you
My friend Georgina have patience.

A STUPID   I didn't know that my husband is a *goat*[1]
HUSBAND   *Iyo oyo ho*
A first husband can afford only *mpanaka*[2]
Give me only enough for cassava chaff
Ayio, Ayio Ayio Oyoho

[1] A goat is a symbol for stupidity, not for lechery as in the
    English tradition.
[2] 'Mpanaka' is a small lamp the framework of which is made
    of an empty milk tin, filled with palm oil. The wick is made
    of any piece of cloth. It is the cheapest type of lamp, worth
    about three pence.

[66]

I didn't know that my husband is a *beast*[1]
    Iyio oyo ho
Please don't crush the baby as you lie
Give money only enough for cassava chaff.

COUNCIL MEN   A message should be taken to the Council men
        at Aboh
Should the ruling of this world be with guns?
Should it be with matchets?
Before Licence is due
They drive around in cars
You get to Afọ Oru
They block the road with their cars
A young man comes to market
They beat him up and throw him in the van
Council men
Are you telling us to leave off trading?
Are you telling us to go make bullets?

GOVERNMENT'S   The promise of Government at the beginning:
PROMISE   Anybody in a ditch who holds out his hand
Will get a share of Government's amenities
Ezinihitte, kingly men, have held out their hand
Share of government amenities is now due
Do we not belong to the party at Enugu?
We have no wide road leading to the market
We have no pump water to slake our thirst
Pity! (Alas!)
The census counting is not clear to us.

[1]   The man is a beast because he cannot control his passion.

7 LAMENTATION POEMS

translated by D. I. Nwoga

SAVIOUR	Saviour of those in difficulty, mother
(a)	Road to the stream never without soap, mother
	Shop where cloths are displayed, mother
	Joy of the married state, mother
	Beautiful house where wealth is preserved, mother
	Great mother of young children, mother
	She that cooks in a great pot, mother
	Don't you see, your fellow women have arrived
	Ozirigbo[1] used in your enthroning, is it still there I ask?
	Somebody please play the *ozirigbo*, let me see if she will come.

(b) Engine head that shakes the earth, my big mother,
Your fellow women are mourning
Today it is a year since we have searched for you
We have searched and have not found her
We haven't seen her, Mother, Saviour of those in difficulty.
Please start our dance,[2] let us see whether she will come[3]
Truly, let us see whether she is coming
We finished playing our dance and did not see her
We didn't see our mother;
Don't you see, sleep that lasts a week has become death!

SORROWS When you think of hardships[4] you take drugs.

[1] *Ozirigbo* is a large gong usually played by the leader of the women's dance group.
[2] Literally 'put on our record'. The women consider their dance as good as any phonograph record.
[3] The woman being mourned was patron of the dance group.
[4] *Uwa* by itself is 'the world', but it is very often used as an abbreviation of 'uwa ǫjǫǫ', i.e. a life of frustration and hardships.

[71]

Good friend, to whom shall I speak of my sorrows?
To whom shall I tell my sorrows? Darkness has
   come on me.
Woman that was made a queen, whose children
   were made royal
The world is hard on me
Lolo,[1] first born of my sisters, where has she gone?
Mother, death kills thoughtlessly
Death kills without regard
Why does she who does good deeds die too early
Son of my sister, greatwarrior, owner of my person,
He who listens as he walks has given cause for
   trouble
Truly, Death has injured our hearts
Maurice,[2] elder brother,
Truly, we each have a share in death
I am asking where has my sister gone?
Woman, made a queen by all, where has she gone?
O men, it is a tragedy
O women, it is a tragedy
Oliver, what is not lost is still where it was kept.
High-minded animals are never caught in a trap,
   my people
Come and tell your woes
Come and tell your woes; darkness has descended
   on us
Nothing is wrong among us except that death has
   come on us
It is death that has placed me in this state
Mother, life is hard with me and my enemy
But my enemy glories that mine is harder than his
Alas, for my enemy.

[1]   *Lolo* is a title which had been conferred on the woman
being mourned to honour her for her achievements.
[2]   Maurice was the surviving brother of the dead woman.

Weeping does not end sorrow
Weeping does not end sorrow
Lọlọ, my first born sister, where, I ask, has she
    gone?
We have cried much
I am crying much; life is hard
We speak to the world of the course of events
Death kills thoughtlessly
My first-born sister, *Lọlọ*, death kills thoughtlessly.
O men, it is a disaster
O women, it is a disaster
So she is dead, the woman made queen by all?
Emezioha[1] owner of my person, do be consoled,
Console yourself for it is death
My people, does one ever know what is in the
    minds of others?
I have suffered!
Death that has killed *Lọlọ* had an implacable mind
So she is dead, woman for whom all vibrated in
    joy?
To whom shall I speak of my sorrows?
Whom shall I tell my woes?
Darkness has descended on us.
                    (Abigbo solo recital)

MY SISTER   Death has broken our hearts
LỌLỌ   My sister *Lọlọ*
            Where could she have gone?
            People have cried much
            For women whom she has taught how to work
            What is to be done?
            She taught them how to plant cassava
            She looked after these women

    [1]   Emezioha—the husband of the dead woman is being
            addressed here.

[73]

Taught them how best to make palm oil.
Children of our sister,[1] do not lament
It is death
And we all each have a share in death
Lọlọ thought much for the good of our land
Death gave her not a chance
Death kills thoughtlessly
Death kills without regard
Death kills without wisdom.

**DEATH HAS
CRUSHED MY
HEART**

My brother death has crushed my heart.
My brother has left me at crossroads
My brother has left me hanging over the fire like a
    parcel of meat to dry
But a parcel of meat over the fire will still have
    somebody to touch it.
Death has reaped me up like cocoyam and peeled
    off my tubers
My left hand has turned to my back
Death has turned me into bitterness itself
My mirror is broken
My own is past.[2]

1   *Okele* (in the vernacular version) is the affectionate name by
    which children of a woman are called by any natives of her
    village. It confers certain traditional privileges on the
    children.
2   I am forever doomed.